Y0-CBD-224

THE ENLIGHTENMENT CODE

THE
ENLIGHTENMENT
CODE

FOR RACHEL

TED WENTWORTH

Ted Wentworth
9-19-20

ENLIGHTENMENT LIFESTYLE PRESS
NEWPORT BEACH, CALIFORNIA

Copyright © 2012 by Theodore S. Wentworth. All rights reserved.

Published by Enlightenment Lifestyle Press
2618 San Miguel Drive
Suite 222
Newport Beach, CA 92660
www.EnlightenmentCode.com

No part of this book may be reproduced in any form without permission
in writing from the author, except for brief quotations embodied in critical
articles or reviews.

"Without Brushing My Hair" and "I Have Learned So Much" are
from the Penguin publication *The Gift, Poems by Hafiz,* by Daniel Ladinsky.
Copyright©1999 by Daniel Ladinsky, and used with his permission.

Haiku selections are from the forthcoming publication, *Tattoos on the Buddha,
Haiku the Ink* by Daniel Ladinsky and Nancy Owen Barton.
Copyright©2012 by Daniel Ladinsky, and used with his permission.

Design Kira Fulks | www.kirafulks.com

Cataloging-in-publication data is on file with the Library of Congress.

ISBN: 978-0-9854940-0-1

Printed in the USA

For

Shree Maa
Swami Satyananda Saraswati
and
our Devi Mandir family
and the members of the Inside Edge
(www.InsideEdge.org)

Acknowledgments

The author is deeply grateful
for support and encouragement from the following
(in alphabetical order):

Fred Alvord

Nancy Owen Barton

Michael Coleman

David Fagan

Kira Fulks

Deborah Gaal

Rob Gunther

Floren Harper

Candice Katayama

Bruce and Jennifer Kellogg

Mary Olsen Kelly

Daniel Ladinsky

Carolyn Long

Sandy and Kirk Moore

Tim Piering

Amanda Pisani

Kathy and Court Purdy

Patty Truman

Rama Vernon

CONTENTS

Prologue

Have you, like me, spent a lifetime wondering how to find out who you truly are? Have you wondered if there's a secret code to attaining enlightenment, a sure-footed path into the heart of the Divine? I promise you, there is!

This book is your invitation to join me in exploring the greatest mystery of the Divine. If you'd like to learn about my journey before we begin, read on. If you'd prefer to start unraveling the Enlightenment Code immediately, turn to Chapter One.

Why Trust Me?

As a youth, I considered the totality of the Divine as the infinite, unsolvable enigma, yet over the decades, it's become apparent that certain aspects of the Divine invite knowledge and experience, and do, without doubt, open themselves to inquiry.

It's taken over forty years for me to unlock the codes that hide the mystery of the Divine. I managed to do this as a full-time husband and father and while pursuing a significant professional career. My experience demonstrates that you can have a full family life, a rewarding career, *and* successfully engage in spiritual practice and follow a spiritual path.

HOW MY JOURNEY BEGAN

In my teens I became fascinated when I encountered a philosophy professor who didn't believe in God. I wanted to change his mind, and although I was raised Christian, I began to visit all the holy men I could find—mostly Christian and Jewish. Their advice, in essence, was: "You must believe—you have to have faith." They assured me that faith came from within, and there weren't words powerful enough to convince a nonbeliever.

I saw the professor frequently, and continued my quest to find something that would convince him there was a higher power. Looking back now, nothing I said or showed him seemed to have any effect on his outlook—but then again, I didn't yet know about the Rishis, meditation, or the levels of consciousness.

I wondered if church leaders wanted me to *believe* in the unseen because they couldn't show me how to *feel* and to *know* the unseen. I felt disappointment that the churches I visited didn't offer tools sophisticated enough to create a direct experience. Sure, music and words are beautiful and uplifting, yet I often left church with a hollow feeling, a gnawing *soul hunger*.

Driven to Find Answers

My quest was not solely intellectual. Between the ages of ten and seventeen, I suffered from petit mal seizures. These are also known as "absence" seizures; victims rarely fall down, but they seem to "go blank" for a short period of time. The drugs doctors gave me didn't work, and although the seizures didn't harm me physically, they resulted in a torrent of hurt feelings. I tried to ignore the odd looks I got following an episode—I looked like a normal kid, but I must have appeared very strange.

What I wanted more than anything was for God to heal me, so I prayed a lot. Medicine's failure left me with every reason to do all that I could to know God and cure the seizures so I could live a normal life, drive a car, have a girlfriend, and find meaningful work.

Because my prayers seemed inadequate, I looked for someone with a demonstrable, one-on-one relationship with God to intercede. The only person I could think of was Oral Roberts, the popular TV evangelist known for his "miraculous" cures. I was almost seventeen when I traveled five hundred miles to hear Rev. Roberts speak.

Arriving early, I was rewarded with a place in the "healing line." When my turn came, I stood before Rev. Roberts, and as he placed the palm of his right hand on my forehead, I must have blacked out. The next thing I recall was that someone was standing behind me, gently holding me by my shoulders. I was facing the audience, which was cheering wildly. Within a few seconds I was escorted offstage and down the stairs where I told an aide that I'd blacked out and missed the healing. He told me not to worry and that I should return to my seat. I rode home grief-stricken at what I assumed was yet another failure. Had I just blown my last chance to be healed?

Two days after arriving home, however, I noticed I didn't have a seizure. Every few months I might go a day without an episode, but never two days in row. And then the third day came and went. None! And none since to this day.

Now, years later, I can see how the blackouts brought me into an intimate connection with the Divine, and how they were responsible for my immense curiosity and determination. They taught me that answers become available when I commit to do whatever is necessary to find them.

A Decade of Doing

With the discontinuance of the seizures, a whole new life opened up for me. College followed, then law school at University of California's Hastings College of Law in San Francisco, a very tough school where one-third of the students were tossed out by the end of the first year. The challenges were huge, but nothing stopped me, and by the age of twenty-four I had my JD from Hastings and was admitted to the California bar.

I had no idea where to set down roots and practice, but I did know that I was crazy for sailing and wanted to go south to a warmer climate. Sensing I would "know" the place when I saw it, I started looking for an apartment when I got to Southern California's Newport

Beach. Within two weeks, I had moved in and secured a job with the only personal injury law firm in Orange County. When the firm split up in my fourth year of practice, two of the senior partners and I stayed on. We became Hunt, Liljestrom and Wentworth, an A-rated litigation firm. During those years I was busily engaged in professionally establishing myself, and in 1965, I met and married my lovely next-door neighbor, Sharon Arkush.

My questions about God and religion were never overshadowed by my other pursuits. I'd had a meeting with the Divine that had radically changed my life, yet I'd somehow missed the actual experience. Believe me, that wasn't going to happen again.

SPIRITUAL DOORS OPEN

In 1970, I was thirty-one years old and contentedly married with two little girls when I became an active seeker once again. Like most Westerners forty years ago (and many today, in spite of the yoga studios on every Main Street), I had reservations about Eastern beliefs and spiritual practices. But my curiosity was stronger than my skepticism, and I attended a lecture on Transcendental Meditation at the University of California, Irvine. I was deeply impressed—not only with the amazing information I was getting about the "anatomy of consciousness," but with the program itself. This wasn't some wacky practice being promoted by a bunch of hippies. A respected world-class Master (with a degree in physics) had devised a carefully guided curriculum that was being scientifically followed and evaluated. Because I could support this, and trust it intellectually, I dove in.

Within a week, my wife Sharon and I were receiving instruction in TM from a teacher trained by Maharishi Mahesh Yogi. Over the following five years, I studied and meditated with great devotion, and, evaluating my progress every six months, felt satisfied with my growth. But as you've probably experienced yourself, spiritual development isn't something that you cozily settle into. I didn't know what *more* was, but I wanted it. By 1975, I knew to take a new step on the path.

I felt to really learn and experience more, and to do it fully, I needed to travel to India. But I was unwilling to leave my practice and my wife and two daughters. Fortunately, I had the good fortune to meet a man named Dale, who was very knowledgeable about spiritual paths. He and I shared a deep spiritual curiosity and were both eager to pursue our quest for understanding the esoteric aspects of the Divine. I decided to sponsor Dale as a traveling emissary to explore the world on my behalf. Dale would go wherever was necessary to meet experts who could answer our questions, like "Who's becoming enlightened?" and "How are they doing it?" We were also curious about whether meditation was really necessary. Wasn't there a faster way?

INVESTIGATING THE ORIGINS

Over the next seven years, Dale was traveling while I continued meditating and studying the ancient Vedas. These are the sacred books of the Hindu and Buddhist religions written by the Rishis, spiritual Masters who intuitively cognized the Vedas more than ten thousand years ago. To our surprise, our research proved without a doubt that *all* religions have blossomed from the Vedas. And we realized there is a vast difference between religion (an institutionalized system of beliefs) and spirituality (a personal and experiential quest, following a carefully chosen path to directly experience the Divine). We were interested in the latter, and sought paths that are real and pure, and that could deliver as represented.

We found only a limited number of recognized traditions whereby devotees could reasonably expect to find, and to experience, what we call enlightenment. Why, we asked ourselves, did there seem to be an ancient bottleneck on understanding enlightenment?

Delving into history, we found that the path to spiritual knowledge and advancement contains many secrets, such as the science of sound and the science of breath, both of which I will explore with you later. Such secrets are kept because not every seeker has the experience and judgment to use such information wisely, and powerful techniques can be counterproductive if they are used before a devotee has gained a certain level of development and devotion. (Imagine a first-year engineering student attempting to build a hundred-story building from scratch. Kiss that building good-bye!)

We learned that information and more advanced techniques become available from appropriate teachers who "magically" appear along the seeker's path. Gurus are gurus for a reason—they guide devotees' training, exposing advanced techniques when the time is right, so they progress in an orderly and safe manner, at their own speed, step-by-step.

As we studied, and experienced expanding consciousness, the years flew by. During this time I decided to take a three-month "sabbatical," in order to immerse myself in sacred study. My partners at the law firm made it clear that they would never grant me even half that much time off. But as you know by now, I am devoted and determined. I had a great position and career, yet Sharon and I agreed that considering our adequate savings, leaving my partners was a risk worth taking. So in November 1977, I walked away from the "safety" of my law practice. I had time to immerse myself in sacred study, and when I was ready, I opened a solo practice, the Law Offices of Theodore S. Wentworth. With my own business, I was able to balance my spiritual and professional life so I was not overcommitted.

INDIA, FINALLY

Dale and I were finishing our world research when in 1983 I was invited to India by one of Dale's contacts, Ravi, a spiritual teacher. During our phone conversation Ravi assured me that when I arrived he would introduce me to at least eight to ten Masters. I travelled to India for a three-week stay. While there, doors to an entirely new world opened to me.

Almost thirty years ago, after years of sacred study and research, I arrived in Kolkata (Calcutta) India. Within eight hours I felt drawn, even compelled, to visit the historic Dakshineswar temple where the great sage Paramahansa Ramakrishna, a true avatar, lived his entire adult life.

Just stepping onto the grounds I felt the familiarity of home. I could sense Ramakrishna's presence in the temple, and the rooms in which the great Master lived captured me. Most of my time in Kolkata was spent at that temple. The strength of the connection I felt at Dakshineswar was greater than I can describe, and my experience there became a defining moment along my path. Years later I would discover why.

On leaving Kolkata, Dale and I departed for the southern part of the country to stay as honored guests in the family home of the man who had invited me to India.

Dakshineswar Temple

What followed deeply affected my heart. Every day brought new revelations. Hiring a car and driver, Dale, Ravi, Ravi's dad, and I traveled southwestern India visiting one Master after another. All knew Ravi and greeted him with respect. (Ravi would in time become, and remains today, one of the world's most beneficent Masters, Shri Shri Ravi Shankar.)

Dale and I then traveled alone to northern India with instructions from Ravi on where to go and whom to see. He made arrangements for us to be welcomed, so our northern trip was astonishing. We were on the inside path, meeting ten Masters who would never have been available to a couple of unknown devotees from California. I learned volumes during this visit—so many secrets, more than I can tell you yet. Those meetings with well-established Masters launched me even further into a lifetime of spiritual advancement.

No one would have predicted, especially myself, that a disabled kid facing a very limited lifestyle would one day be welcomed into such company. I'm so grateful to have had these opportunities.

You will see it was traits honed by divine adversity that made all the difference. Through my deep curiosity and my determination to uncover hidden causes, I've risen far beyond what seemed insurmountable, to the point that I've become known for my ability to bust the mystery behind events—no matter how long it takes. And, it doesn't matter how complex the mystery—if it's on my plate I never give up. I made my living as a trial attorney, and it was this persistence, curiosity, and insight that landed me on *The Oprah Winfrey Show* and many leading national news programs.

Busting secrets sometimes requires solving tangled layers of threads that have to be "unraveled" before they can be reorganized to reveal the solution. My trip to India offered the clarity of mind to reassemble much of what I'd been learning. As I said, the trip opened many doors for me. At the same time, another door was closing.

The Divine Story Cuts Deep

Sadly, a month after my return home, Sharon was diagnosed with terminal cancer. My studies—everything—took a backseat, as healing her became my new priority. Within a few months it became clear there would be no arguing with the divine plan and timing for Sharon to transition. Sharon, my wife of twenty-two years and the mother of our children, was also my best friend. Her passing was enormously painful and it launched me onto an amazing path paved with destiny.

Those of you familiar with my first book, *Build a Better Spouse Trap*, know that through determination and the formation of a spiritual strategy, two years later I was blessed to meet and marry another remarkable woman—Diana von Welanetz. Diana too had lost her spouse to cancer, and the romantic and spiritual story of how we found each other is in her popular book *Send Me Someone: A True Story of Love Here and Hereafter* [http://tinyurl.com/3hhnomd].

A GREAT MASTER

I married Diana in December 1989; we had so much in common—we'd both been meditating for nearly twenty years. Our shared spiritual practice took a new direction in the mid-90s when a somewhat unbelievable number of "coincidences" intersected our lives with that of Shree Maa of Kamakhya. Soon we were visiting with Shree Maa and her associate, Swami Satyananda Saraswati (Swamiji) at her ashram, Devi Mandir, in Northern California. Our profound relationship with Shree Maa and Swamiji continues to this day, and we've been close to them now for fifteen years. We both found the intimate relationship with world-class enlightened Masters that we'd always longed for.

SHREE MAA'S GRACE, GIFTS FOR ALL

So, before my story ends, I want to tell you that yes, I visit all the levels of enlightenment that I spent my life seeking. Through forty years of meditating and study I've found a way to not only *experience* divinity, but to spark that awareness in others.

I have many direct experiences every day... and while my inclination is to simply savor the wonders, Shree Maa and Swamiji have now commanded me to share with you all that I know. And so, with this book, I honor their request by bringing you the Vedic path I follow—a "holy shortcut," if you will—into the heart of the Divine.

*Lassoing Buddha
wasn't easy, but my
options ran out.*

Daniel Ladinsky

THE ENLIGHTENMENT CODE

CHAPTER ONE

THE NATURE OF THE UNIVERSE: SEEN AND UNSEEN

In this book I will share with you sacred and subtle information about the true nature of the universe—both the universe we see and the universe that is not visible to the eye.

In my experience, when assimilating knowledge (as opposed to reading a novel) the more succinct the presentation, the easier it is to understand. So, with your indulgence, I'll do my best to be as brief and concise as possible.

For discussions related to human destiny, Vedic wisdom tells us the universe is composed of three worlds. The worlds are not linear or separated by space or distance; rather, they permeate everything including one another and realms more dense than their own. It's possible for us to experience them as progressive layers of subtlety, stillness, and *silence* within us.

Three Connected Worlds

The first is the physical world—body, mind, and ego—the material world of the five senses we're familiar with from our everyday experience in the awakened state.

The second is the mental world. Quieting our mind and body takes us within, where we've transcended beyond thought, beyond the material world—the world of matter and our senses. Our sensory perception adjusts to the new level of growing subtlety, stillness and silence, similar to how eyes adjust to the dark. Here we encounter a subtle plane where we experience mental images, expanded feelings of love, bliss, increased creativity, and expanded intuition. But no thoughts! When we find ourselves beyond thought, what's left? Welcome to the gateway to the third world and high Consciousness.

The third world is the causal world, the unimaginable, magnificent world of the Divine. As our inner awareness relaxes and deepens, releasing its attachments to the material world, our capacity to dive deeper into subtle consciousness continues to refine, carrying our awareness beyond and into the sacred world of the Divine. I have a lot to share with you about this third world that is so much more *real* and more present than the physical world with its endless illusions.

RELIABLE AUTHORITY

My understanding of the nature of the universe is confirmed by the Vedas,[1] the ancient texts of the Golden Age. The four Vedas are the most extraordinary artifact researchers have from the ancient past, and it's generally agreed that they are the most comprehensive and universal of all ancient scriptures.

I regard the Vedas, rather than material science, technology, or religious rhetoric, as the ultimate and final authority in the field of the Divine.

The Vedas were initially visualized in 7300 BCE, nearly ten thousand years ago, by the Rishis, a group of enlightened sages (seers of sacred sounds called mantras, and all of creation) who lived in India. In addition to cognizing the Vedas, the Rishis also served to maintain the consciousness of the Vedas and to preserve the principles and purity of the teachings over time. That's how the Vedas withstood the long, dark period of recent history. Their depth and absence of ambiguity became the source of all Western languages and were instrumental in the development of all religions. *Yes, all* religions have drawn source material from the Vedas.

---

[1] The Vedas are composed of four ancient texts: the Rig Veda, Atharva Veda, Yajur Veda, and Sama Veda.

Science as Authority

I know that it's considered unthinkable to reject the assertions of science in its explanation of the universe. Yet we simply can't rely on science when it comes to spiritual matters. Science is but a window through which human intellect and politics peek in their attempt to define whatever issue is before them. It's worth noting that researchers *invent*, science just explains and *defines*. The great limitation of science is "the scientific method," which holds that "if the findings don't replicate—they are not verifiable." Science is thus empowered to disregard most of the content of the immeasurable subtle worlds and label them as unscientific, unproven, and doubtful.

Proof

The very existence of miracles and unexplained mysteries is proof that the subtle worlds are beyond science's understanding of the laws of nature.

Energy

One theoretical physicist who thought outside the traditional confines of science was Albert Einstein. Einstein confirmed the universe is an infinite sea of energy and consciousness, and he confirmed that there is only one Energy—which cannot be created or destroyed—it can only be changed from one form to another.

Einstein's formula, E=mc2 demonstrates that the entire universe is Energy and that mass and energy are equal and interchangeable. Science acknowledges this infinite conscious Energy as "the unified field."

For our purposes, I'd like to temporarily name this infinite, conscious Energy, *It*. *It* is every aspect of the physical, mental, and causal worlds I spoke of earlier.

IT

As is apparent from the text of the Vedas, the ancient Rishis long ago intuitively cognized an "infinite sea of energy and consciousness." The Rishis had, moreover, the ability to *become* the Energy and because of their omnipresence, to move anywhere in time and report back on their findings. They have told us that not only is *It* infinite, ageless, and conscious, *It* has intention, intelligence, compassion, omnipresence, omniscience, and omnipotence. Simply, *It* is *pure* Energy that assumes any form, anywhere. The Rishis found that because *It* is *everything*, it is impossible to name, to pray to, to seek help from, or to worship. Accordingly, they are said to have invited this Divine Energy to make *It*self more available to, and knowable by, the human race.

ONE BECOMES MANY

The Vedas tell us how, with great love, *It*, the Godhead, the divine source of Being through which all emanates, divided *It*self into many aspects, attributes, natures, and qualities.

Male and female became apparent. Consciousness—the pure, silent, male attribute, is the unmanifest aspect of the Divine associated with absolute stillness and silence. Sometimes known as "Father," this aspect was given the Vedic Sanskrit name, *Shiva*.

Action—the female attribute, is the manifest aspect and constitutes all action, physical energy, and form. Sometimes known as "Mother," or "Mother Nature," this aspect was given the Vedic Sanskrit name, *Shakti*. (Sanskrit, a very precise language, was created to prevent ambiguity and convey the subtle nuances of Consciousness.)

Over time, the unmanifest aspect of *It* has divided again and again, and been given new names. Religions developed, language evolved, and understandings of *It* spread from country to country. Hindu divisions, for instance, include the deities of Brahma, Lakshmi, Kali, and Krishna along with many more; Christians worship God as a trilogy, Father, Son and Holy Ghost, in addition to Mother Mary along with many saints; Muslims have one Deity, Allah; the Hebrews have their One god, Yahweh. And, of course, Buddhists revere Buddha as the first enlightened human.

GOD OF ALL

And so, *It* is recognized by the population of our planet by numerous "nicknames"—including, God, Tao, Yahweh, Elohim, Brahma, and Jehovah. (Doesn't every important thing have many names? Water, *agua*, *wasser*—whatever the name—it's all the same. As Shakespeare wrote: "What's in a name? That which we call a rose by any other name would smell as sweet.")

Accordingly, we have one God, worshiped differently by the devotees of many religions. Each religion offers a unique manner of fulfilling the love of God through the needs and temperament of its souls and their culture.

In every house of worship, all I see are people loving God. My heart is swept with them—into the same God I love. All of us dancing in our own way to the same music, each learning to bebop in the void. There are seven billion souls on earth, seven billion individual paths to the Divine—the one and only Energy of the universe.

WHAT IS GOD?

All religions agree that the one Divine Energy is omnipresent. That means *It*'s everywhere, and if God is everywhere and everything, then every atom—with its subatomic parts—is nothing less than the Divine *It*self. And because all physical forms are made up of atoms, Nature's only building blocks, there is no form, large or small, that *isn't It*. Even Einstein, remember, agrees.

The secret is: Consciousness, the unmanifest, male aspect of the Divine—when slipped into a container—perfectly and completely identifies with its container. That means the consciousness in a rock, "thinks" it's a rock, like the air in a balloon might "think" it's the balloon, and the water in a vase might "think" it's the vase.

Thus, the feminine aspect (all form and action) is everything we see around us. All form is simply our male aspect (Consciousness) masquerading as a container—you, me, a shoelace, a building, a button—or a puppy dog tail. It's the containers that cause us to feel separate, but you can now see that the container is but an illusion.

Again, the male aspect (Consciousness) has merged with (married) the feminine aspect (container) to enjoy *It*self—to enjoy *It*self as the Universe, as the Cosmos, as all of Nature. We, through our containers, are all part of a *story*—the magnificent "play and display" of the Divine.

So, we are God Consciousness—in divine containers. Every container has Consciousness. Containers—all forms are created out of, and from within Her own Being. She, herself, becomes the physical universe. Birthing without a birth canal, She...transforms! Not unlike the way white light, shining through a crystal, becomes a rainbow of seven colors made of the same stuff. The Divine is everything, all forms—everywhere. Just as the waves, foam, and icebergs *are* the ocean—so are we all the Divine—that Energy we call God.

It feels correct to say, "God is *in* everyone"—but it's more accurate to say, "God *is* everyone." *It is* you, *It is* me, and *is* all other animals, trees—and things. The seer and the seen—are One. Divine. *It!*

There is nothing we can perceive, form or formless, physical or spiritual, that is not the intrinsic nature of all, the Supreme Consciousness of all, the Energy of all.

Right now...please stop and look around you and realize that everything you perceive, all of it, has something, *everything,* in common with you—we're not just sharing that One Energy—we all *are* that One Energy—God.

"God dwells within you as you."[2] Please say this deeply profound and empowering truth to yourself, over and over:

"God dwells within me as me,
God dwells within me as me,
God dwells within me as..."

Astonishing, isn't it?

---

[2] This phrase is often attributed to Baba Muktananda of the Siddha Yoga tradition.

WITHOUT BRUSHING MY HAIR

The closer
I get to you, Beloved,
The more I can see
It is just You and I all alone
In this World.

I hear
A knock at my door,
Who else could it be,
So I rush without brushing
My hair.

For too
Many nights
I have begged for Your
Return

And what
Is the use of vanity
At this late hour, at this divine season,
That has now come to my folded
Knees?

If your love letters are true dear God
I will surrender myself to
Who you keep saying
I
Am.

Hafiz

CHAPTER TWO

So, Who Are We Then?

I f we *are* it all—everything—why don't we *know* we're
God? The best answer is the simple one: we don't
know we're God because we are preoccupied and distracted by our containers.

Our containers have an intelligence of their own,
which is attached to the senses, bringing us information
about our surroundings that is extremely distracting. It
is so distracting that even while awake we are unable to
stabilize the mind on a thought without our mind "looking out the window."

AFRAID TO LAUGH

And there is one other reason that we don't know that
we're God. As Voltaire put it: "God is a comedian, play-
ing to an audience too afraid to laugh!" To appreciate this

remark, it's helpful to know that according to the Masters we've interviewed, God has five jobs. They are:

1. Create
2. Maintain
3. Destroy
4. Bestow grace and
5. Hide *Its own existence*!

Try to imagine a player more engaging and dreaded in a game of hide and seek than Mother Divine. She hides in containers that are preoccupied and distracted by something called *maya*.

Maya—That Which Is Not

Maya is a *force*, the curtain of illusion that conceals our divinity. Maya is the source of our distraction, preoccupation, and negativity. It's our drama and our trance of dissatisfaction. Maya serves as the perfect camouflage to hide our true nature.

Our container is a human, an animal body with an intelligence of its own! Maya, as a force, causes our *container*—our animal body and its mind-ego—to react, and to *think*, and to attempt to reason itself to freedom.

Maya is the device through which the Supreme Deity makes one reality appear as the many. It provides individual souls with the "ten thousand things" (the spiritual name for the things that emotionally engage and preoccupy us, and create the mirage of confusion and constant chaos.) It is the stuff that brings about error.

The power of maya, illusion, causes us to see our needs, fears, loves—our cravings—as though they were outside us. It's as though we live on a mirror; all we see is ourselves. And for some of us, our lives are so stressed that we feel confined to a warped, distorted, fun house mirror. Again, the force of maya causes us to perceive only our own "stuff," leading us to act out *our* stuff against others as though it were theirs.

Our ego is habituated to maya and hooked on the stuff that poisons us; stuff we haven't learned to handle, such as: hostility, drama, striving, and comparing. More stuff includes the ignorance of the judgmental ego, it's thoughts, drives, and its own outlandish internal dialog (the monkey mind) that just won't shut up! We are addicted to the mind's dramatization of its fears and fantasies (futuring) and its shames and memories (pasting). We truly are prisoners of our conditioning.

WHO WANTS TO BE UNIQUE?

Maya! What else could it be that makes us all strive to be different, to be special, to be unique? The more aggrandized we are in our own mind, the smaller we become. This endlessly judging, comparing monkey mind overshadows our true nature. Our Oneness! Maya won't even let us "be here now" long enough to sing our national anthem without distraction. Have you noticed we sing with misplaced attention, just mouthing words while preoccupied, watching the peanut vendor or the mom trying to get her kid to stand up and behave? We greet our loved ones, say "Hi, I love you," and hug them, while our attention, again, is preoccupied, worrying over what we have to do tomorrow morning.

If we're not self-aggrandizing; we're self-deprecating. We criticize ourselves for being judgmental of others *and ourselves*. Habitually agitated over too much and too little; we find something wrong with everything. Always, dissatisfaction clouds our heart. In a word—suffering!

THERE'S HOPE...

Meditation is *the* powerful antidote to maya. Our mind with its wild and crazy thoughts will eventually stabilize if we use an extremely powerful tool—a coded tool that is *invincible.*

I knew something about
The Enlightenment Code when
the moon got naked.

Daniel Ladinsky

CHAPTER THREE

FINDING OUR SOULS

To awaken we must experience the presence of our soul. The soul is one of the first stars to appear as we attain enlightenment.

Our soul serves as the watcher—the witness. When this witness awakens it will also begin to remember, totally changing the way we see and understand our environment and ourselves. Astounding!

MEET YOUR SOUL?

If you haven't met your soul yet, let's do it now. I would ask you:

"What did it feel like to be eight years old?"

"Did you feel older than eight, maybe in your twenties?"

Take a moment now to remember that feeling. (Please, don't just read on, do it...and please don't peek ahead. Take a breath and participate in this little experiment, because there is a 90 percent chance you're going to consciously experience your soul in the next sixty seconds!)

"And now that you are over thirty, don't you feel younger than your years?" Most people, regardless of whether they're eight or fifty-eight, have a sense they are at an age of great vitality and promise—about twenty-two years old.

Follow me here—place your hand over that part of your body that feels older than your years when you were young, and younger than your years now that you are older.[3]

---

[3] Please note: This experiment might not work well for readers who are in their late teens or early twenties. It seems that most people, regardless of their current chronological age, experience their ageless, infinite soul as similar to their sense of their ability when they were about twenty-two. If that's true, then it could be difficult for young adults to experience the contrast between body and soul, although ages seven to fifteen, and ages thirty and older, seem to have no difficulty.

ATMAN

Your hand, of course, moves to your heart. Not your physical heart so much as the energy of your heart center (heart chakra). Your heart center is the seat of your soul (*atman*). You know your soul's there because as your body ages, your deathless, infinite Consciousness, your soul, remains "young at heart."

This Consciousness is you—the Divine that dwells within. Now, perhaps for the first time, you've given it formal recognition, as well as an identity, location, and a Sanskrit name.

When you gain a sense of your soul, and then think about yourself, you probably won't have an image of your mundane daily roles such as man, woman, father, mother, artist, student, homemaker, executive, etc. Rather, you'll identify with your heart energy, your infinite, ageless, God Consciousness within.

This slightest awareness of infinite Consciousness fills you with a sense of how capable your consciousness is of expanding far beyond your present experience.

So close I had to come
to hear God whisper
what I wanted

Daniel Ladinsky

CHAPTER FOUR

REBIRTH: THE WHEEL OF LIFE

When our bodies quit, our Consciousness is freed from its container as it shuts down. Our infinite, ageless Energy (soul) remains intact, recycling through the Divine to return in another body. This cycle of birth, death, and rebirth is called "the wheel of life."

Freed from their earthly container, our souls return "home"[4] (a state of Being, not unlike heaven) for rest and reevaluation between lives. While home, our Consciousness is free of any container. We find ourselves in a realm that suits our temperament, and our Consciousness is very much self-aware and awake.

---

[4] I regard the word "heaven" to be an emotional trigger. As such, it might well make the information I'm wanting to convey more difficult to assimilate. Attempting to resolve this issue, I have substituted the word "home."

THE NEED TO REINCARNATE

If home is such a reward, so refreshing, wouldn't you think that we'd stay there all the time? And we could, if in our past incarnations our souls had not acquired baggage that instills the desire to reincarnate. This baggage is made up of unresolved impressions or *samskaras*.

In other words, we can *go* home, but without owning the harmony of innocence and bliss Consciousness, we are not comfortable *remaining* there. Even at home, we are still restless from the lingering effects of habit, hostility, and unfulfilled desires from previous lives.

During each earth life we live a new story and have the opportunity to culture divine virtues and sacred qualities to neutralize the baggage—the residual thoughts, anger, jealousy, and feelings of deprivation. The soul's home experience, tainted by inharmonious desires that are incompatible with home and our highest selves, render the soul so uncomfortable at home that we will choose to return for another incarnation.

HIGH SCHOOL

Don't you think you eliminated a bunch of samskaras during your high school years? In fact, during your high school years, you added a few new samskaras as well. Notice the samskaras weren't eliminated through intention or achievement. We had experiences that neutralized aspects of our residual anger, jealousy, and feelings of deprivation or striving, and they simply disappeared.

The experience of being human prevents us from completely eliminating our total burden of samskaras. It's worth noting that we cannot intellectually lift ourselves out of the cycle; we cannot decide to "escape" it—as humans, we are not that highly evolved. Better to just live well and let the Divine melt away our samskaras. That Grace, remember, is one of *Its* jobs.

So whatever we are afraid of, or whatever we hate, is fertile ground for creating samskaras. For example, an athlete who is terror stricken by the idea of being seriously injured, who stresses about how horrible it would be if he were handicapped, might well attract a handicapped lifetime, as well as its opposite the following lifetime, when his desire to excel as a great athlete becomes a reality.

Similarly, anger, dislike, or lack of neutrality toward any ethnic or religious group is a good way to create a samskara for returning as exactly what you fear or dislike.

A lifetime of deeply understanding and loving the group serves to melt those samskaras so as not to impair your future enlightenment.

The Life We Wanted

It's likely that the bodily experience we're having now is one we longed for in a past lifetime, and our next life will probably be one we longed for while in our present body.

Each Life an Opportunity

Each venture into a new human lifetime is our chance to free ourselves from unresolved impressions, to ascend the sacred ladder of purity, rather than be held back as impure in a pure realm.

There is no way to "achieve." We can only work on surrendering to the practice of love and patience, trusting that purity will quiet the mind and intellect. The remaining silence exposes the divine spark within us—like stars become visible at sundown.

Home is not a proving ground. All our work to improve, and to move from one state of consciousness to the next (which I'll describe in a few pages), must be accomplished on earth.

THE PRICE OF SPINACH

We might be inclined to look at our human lives as drudgery, or even punishment for our ignorance. I love to paraphrase how Guru Dev, one of the great Rishis, and Maharishi Mahesh Yogi's Master, spoke about how exceptional it is to have a human life on earth:

> To get a human body is a rare thing—make full use of it. There are four million kinds of lives that a soul can gather. After that, one gets a chance to be human, to get a human body. Therefore, one should not waste this chance. Every second in human life is very valuable. If you don't value it, then you will have nothing in hand, and you will weep in the end. Because you are human, God has given you power to think and discern what is good and bad. Therefore, you can choose the best possible kind of action.

> You should never consider yourself weak or a fallen creature. Whatever may have happened up to now may be because you didn't realize, but now be careful…

> After attaining a human body, if you don't attain God, then you have sold a diamond at the price of spinach.

OUR DIVINITY

Our lives, samskaras and all, are precious! They are rich with opportunity to learn, to love, and to align with the Divine from which we will awaken into our divinity. Returning to earth in a new body, we can improve our character and temperament. We get a new chance to further evolve our consciousness and in turn, to melt more completely into the Divine.

And, while we can't rationally rid our souls of samskaras, I offer a trustworthy map to hasten the journey to our highest selves. I'll share it with you in a few pages.

The Enlightenment Code,
my breath, my tender gaze
upon any creature.

Daniel Ladinsky

CHAPTER FIVE

LEVELS OF CONSCIOUSNESS

While our experience in form is clouded by illusion, (see Chapter Two), the human container we occupy is capable of culturing its nervous system to hold seven states of consciousness. The highest, or seventh level of consciousness is considered synonymous with enlightenment.

Truly, it's one thing to talk about and describe these states, and it's another to open into them. Such states can't be accurately described, and they are often so subtle, especially when first experienced, that we may need a Master to confirm their presence.

For the purposes of our discussion, let's assume that the first three levels of consciousness are automatic, meaning they are just normal, everyday consciousness with varying levels of awareness indigenous to a human body. Levels four through seven are progressively higher states, cultured, developed and acquired through spiritual discipline (*sadhana*).

The First State: Deep, dreamless sleep.

The Second State: Dreaming sleep.

The Third State: Stressed, daydreaming consciousness. In the third state, our monkey mind spins its internal dialog. It's mired in maya. It has a lot to say about stories—right and wrong, who did what to whom and why, comparisons, judgments, and one-upsmanship—so our attention is distracted and preoccupied with everything external.

> *To a mind that is still—the whole universe surrenders.*
> **~Lao Tzu**

The Fourth State: Doorway to enlightenment.
Once our mind experiences an absence of thought, what's left? If there are no thoughts, isn't that close to being as clean as it gets? The absence of thought leaves no noise to obscure the heart. The sacred mantra (see Chapter Eight on mantras) has cultured and opened our heart exposing a fourth level of consciousness bearing

many names, including transcendence, equipoise, equanimity, and in Sanskrit, *turiya*.

For months, repeating our "so simple it's underrated" meditation experience twice a day, we gradually gain the capacity for the mind to maintain an increasing measure of profound silence. At some point we don't lose our expanding divinity when opening our eyes, reawakening our senses, and then returning to activity.

Awakening from the fourth level into a quiet mind and super-thin ego, we begin to see through the lens of the heart. We are then "witnessing" (noticing the contrast between our body and soul) and are aware of a sense of knowing, remembering, and feelings of bliss Consciousness, love, and expanding joy. We also discern very subtle changes in our consciousness, which over time will become so stable that we are able to recognize the fifth state. Tears of happiness and gratitude are not uncommon.

The Fifth State: Cosmic Consciousness (*savikalpa samadhi*).

Within a state of Cosmic Consciousness, the world is seen very differently from how we perceive it through the ego. We notice that we can "alternate" our consciousness back and forth between viewing through the lens of the soul (heart) and through the eyes of the ego. Truly, we have one foot on earth, and the other in heaven-on-earth.

At this level, we experience the Divine in the subtle world of the soul as omnipresent, absolute, and the embodiment of unconditional love. Our emerging divinity experiences this profound love and everything *as* One—ourselves!

In a mature state of Cosmic Consciousness, for the most part, subtlety has fallen away and we are, effortlessly and obviously, "here and now." We experience what those words mean and are frequently in a state of wonder. "Hmmm, look at this, I am the embodiment of love, and, I *am* the here and now! No one ever told me—hmmm, how silent, how still, how amazing! I have no fear, and make no bargains with the Divine. I simply have perfect knowing into what is happening, and it's obvious I am a Being who has no needs. My merchant relationship with God is gone!" ("Our Father, gimme this, Our Father I know you love me, I need *this* and that too. I'll put an extra $20.00 in the collection plate if you will do this for me." We all have our own version of bargaining with God.) In Cosmic Consciousness, all manipulation falls away, and our dialog becomes our own version of "Lord teach me how to come even closer." "Everything—the street, the people, the buildings, and cars—everything is *me*. Now I understand what 'I am that' is referring to."

In Cosmic Consciousness we experience everything we place our attention on *as* ourselves! We come to realize that we *are* our attention and everything we focus our attention upon. All the emotions of *yearning, deserving,* and *striving* are gone, and what appears in their place is insight after amazing insight. It is a miraculous and astonishing level of awareness, accompanied by the Eternal Bliss of Consciousness, love and profound gratitude. As we become adept in this fifth level, Cosmic Consciousness automatically ripens or matures into a sixth state.

The Sixth State: God Consciousness (enhanced *savikalpa samadhi*).

In the sixth state, everything is God—an experience famous as being impossible to describe. I am God, the road and all the cars are…there is no "road," and there are no "cars." All in existence is seen—is not *seen*—is *experienced* as God.

God Consciousness! Since everything is experienced as God, nothing seems to have a name. Shortly, this sixth state matures, allowing us to progressively lose the experience of "I"…which anchors us in the seventh state.

The Seventh State: Unity Consciousness (*nirvikalpa samadhi*—Master of the Divine).

The "I" in "I am experiencing and knowing God in everything I do and see" melts away leaving us in the seventh state of Consciousness, oneness with the Divine, Pure Being, Unity. Enlightened, we're immersed in *nirvikalpa samadhi*! We no longer *have* joy and love; we *are* joy and love. We experience varying degrees of omniscience, omnipresence, and omnipotence, yet this is not the end. Now our work has just begun.

GOODBYE UNRESOLVED IMPRESSIONS— SAMSKARAS

Samskaras tend to bloom like seeds thrown on fertile soil. If we heat seeds in the oven for a few minutes before casting them upon the lawn they will never sprout. And so it is, when our consciousness rests in Unity, that persistence and the heat (*tapas*) of our devotion has baked our samskaras and neutralized maya.

There are no samskaras remaining to compel a new incarnation, and Unity itself verifies that all karma has been resolved. Unity Consciousness is the key to everything. You are free! While you remain on earth, you will delight in the glory of 200 percent of life.

TWO HUNDRED PERCENT OF LIFE

Enjoying 200 percent of life means that you will have "one foot in heaven and the other on earth." You are able to switch feet (states of consciousness) in seconds.

Your accomplishment is exceptional. You are awake in reality and the embodiment of love. Expect beauty around you. Your huge heart for everything feels amazingly natural because the truth is, you have normalized.

"Pocket miracles" happen in your presence every day—and as amazing as they are, they feel normal. Major miracles occur as needed. The very existence of miracles is simply proof that we don't yet understand all the laws of Nature.

Your job now is to stay in devotion and gratitude. Love the world, and learn to be astonished! Now let's end this discussion and for good reason—the less we talk about matters detailing the subtle life, the better our experiences will be. Dissecting spiritual matters tends to drag them into the physical world. To maintain power and discrimination, it's best we not contaminate the subtle world with the mundane.

Trust that the path is accessible and that following it will get you there.

CHAPTER SIX

THE PATHS TO HIGHER CONSCIOUSNESS

In our journey to expanded consciousness, there are two broad routes from which to choose: the yogic and the tantric. These two paths originated in India, with teachers and texts dating back to the Rishis and the Vedas of more than ten thousand years ago.

THE YOGIC PATH

The yogic tradition is a path of absolute purity and, as such, requires taking vows as a renunciate or monastic, disclaiming and renouncing the entire world except for spiritual practice and ritual (*sadhana,* in Sanskrit), and of course, breath and food. The renunciate surrenders to God, giving up the earth with all its temptations and charms, and practices meditation and sadhana continually. This path is austere and requires continuing sacrifice.

THE TANTRIC PATH

The path of the tantric tradition requires no renunciation as such. We enter this tradition by choosing a teacher who accepts us as we are. Tantric devotees realize that they are in transition, acknowledging, "I am as clean as I am, and I pray God will accept me as I am." The paths of Ralph Waldo Emerson and Henry David Thoreau, two of this country's best-known transcendentalists, were tantric, along with those of most Western mystics leading up to the present. And it is my path as well. Tantric practitioners learn purity on the "installment plan"— attaining purity one step at a time.

EASTERN MASTERS

The first Eastern Master teaching in the West was Swami Vivekananda, Ramakrishna's emissary who lit up America's spirituality when he spoke at the Chicago World's Fair in 1893. I believe he was the first renowned renunciate to offer teachings of the tantric tradition to Western students.

Paramahansa Yogananda, author of the immensely popular *Autobiography of a Yogi*, was enlightened by his brilliant Master, Sri Yukteswar—Rishi, yogi, Vedic educator, astronomer, and futurist—who revered the texts of both the Bhagavad Gita and the Bible. Yogananda was a renunciate who brought the tantric tradition to the West, establishing several Self-Realization Centers, and sparking further interest in more hundreds of thousands.

We are all most familiar with another Eastern Master, Maharishi Mahesh Yogi, a Rishi and yogic renunciate, renowned for devising the Transcendental Meditation (TM) program. Following enlightenment by his Master, he taught the tantric path to millions of devotees around the world with his message that you needn't change your lifestyle, or even give up your vices, all you need to do is meditate twice a day.

He spoke about yogic purity and taught it at his ashrams and centers, but the overall message and teaching was consistent with the tantric path. He carefully designed his courses and lectures around the tantric theme—not only because the tantric path works, but because he saw that Western "householders," (those who live in the world while cultivating the highest consciousness through sacred practices) were not culturally suited to purify themselves through renunciation.

TANTRA AND SEXUALITY

I'm asked occasionally why the word "tantra" is often equated with sexuality. Tantra's *Kama Sutra* is an ancient Sanskrit guide to virtuous living and family life. Only a small portion of the text discusses the nature of love and pleasure—including sexual practices. Times have changed, attitudes have evolved, and Consciousness has vastly expanded since the *Kama Sutra* was written in 200 AD. For instance, in the West, wives are now regarded as equals and partners rather than property. And…sexual standards have so radically changed over the past eighteen hundred years.

In conclusion, abstinence from sexual relations is clearly not required for spiritual advancement on the tantric path. I feel certain that householders of the West will find the *Kama Sutra* neither instructive nor relevant to their spiritual practice.

WHICH PATH IS EASIER?

Neither the yogic nor the tantric path is easy, and both require dedication and devotion. But I favor the tantric path of the householder over what I imagine to be the wrenching hardships and frustration from suppressed desire required of the renunciate.

There is so much more that can be written about the two paths. But now is the time to apply the principle: "if it's not simple, it's not a solution!"[5]

The solution *is* simple. Westerners are not suited to the path of the renunciate, whereas we are obviously ideally suited to the tantric path.

GIVE UP NOTHING

For over forty years my program has been part of the tantric tradition, and I have made a lot of friends along the way. While discussing our experiences, we've noticed that we didn't "give up" anything—we simply lost interest in it. Over the years we watched with some amusement the gradual disappearance of everything impure. Negative habits, qualities, and attachments just evaporated on their own. This is great testimony for the deep and almost magical power of sacred mantra meditation—you won't start out pure, but you will finish up pure enough to become enlightened.

---

[5] Principle of Occam's Razor, also known as the principle of economy.

TIMES CHANGE

The complex tantric practices of old were designed for a different mind, a mind capable of living in dark ages! I seriously doubt any of the great Masters of the past one hundred years ever offered their devotees the ancient, esoteric tantric tools you might find if you researched the subject.

The rules of the past two thousand years have been modernized greatly in the last fifty years, as have new attitudes, language, and technology. We are not turning our back on our origin; we are very simply using the Vedic tools that Thoreau, Emerson, and many modern Westerners discovered to be amazingly valuable and expansive.

Such simpler methodology awakens our cognition and perception, and reduces the time necessary to acquire a divine heart. It works! Best of all, it performs predictably, regardless of our faith of origin.

SIMPLE DOES IT

I cannot emphasize strongly enough—you will expand and evolve through many positive changes during your first three years of practice. You will return over and over again to your faith of origin and observe how its practitioners don't seem to get the meaning of the hymns they are singing or experience what they are saying. You will see clearly that you have not only grown to experience the Divine from deep within, but now find a new depth in the teachings and books you encountered before you set foot on this path. Yet, as satisfied as you find yourself to be...you want more! The mind always wants more.

FOLLOW YOUR HEART

Your heart is your guide, your *guru,* the remover of the darkness of ignorance as you open and radiate your evolving Divine Consciousness into the world. Your heart is indeed your key to invincibility, the key to every doorway ahead.

A divine flame
wanting to appear
made us candles.

Daniel Ladinsky

CHAPTER SEVEN

THE PRACTICE OF MEDITATION

Whether one chooses the yogic or the tantric path, the practice of meditation[6] is the primary method one must employ to arrive at higher states of consciousness. Cosmic Consciousness and beyond is not attainable through the intellect because the mind cannot experience or understand God.

Reading books about God and god stuff may encourage the mind to realize that it's safe for it to surrender to the heart, but ultimately, reading just provides

---

[6] Meditation is different from contemplation and concentration. Contemplation occurs when we quiet ourselves and think or reflect upon a particular concept including spiritual matters, such as the contents of this book. Contemplation involves the intellect, which involves the ego. It does little to quiet the mind and the ego, or strengthen the soul. Concentration is similar, in that it focuses the intellect on a specific thing. It is only the powerful silence of meditation that quiets the mind and the ego, and strengthens the soul.

one with a stronger intellect. The only sure way through the maze of maya and into a direct experience with the Deity is through settling down, quieting the mind and ego, and strengthening the soul. The Divine is found in the silence.

RAJA YOGA

Meditation is a specific, mechanical process using a sacred mantra as a powerful tool. It's the royal or kings way (Raja yoga)[7] to quiet the mind and reveal the Divine. Sacred mantras do the work for us much like a pruning saw removes a small limb—we put the small, very sharp pruning saw in position at the junction of the tree and limb, and then easily guide the saw back and forth, letting the saw "do its thing." Very quickly the limb falls to the ground. Wouldn't you like to dependably and consistently quiet your mind with such ease?

Your sacred mantra (about which I'll elaborate shortly) is as predictable as removing a limb with a sharp saw. Easy and effortless. And if you use the mantra in

---

[7] Kings often had a spiritual Master as part of their court. The Master's duty was to enlighten the king (thus, "your Highness"). The Master's clandestine technique was meditation.

the way in which you will be trained, that process is just as easy and effortless—sit comfortably, close the eyes, and then ease into silently repeating your mantra—back and forth, back and forth—let the mantra "do it's thing."

PRACTICE IS ESSENTIAL

The key to reaping benefits from meditation is meditating regularly. One of the questions we researched worldwide was, "Isn't there an easier, faster way than meditation?" Without exception Masters advised that there are other methods, but meditation offers the speed of a rocket as compared to walking uphill. They also confirmed that we aren't committing to meditate forever, that once nirvikalpa samadhi is achieved, one often chooses to meditate for the sheer bliss of meditating, but the need to meditate for enlightenment is complete.

At the same time the Masters revealed that changes in the cosmos were currently energizing and increasing the effects of our meditation. Only two hundred years ago enlightenment was not a viable option for the householder. That's the main reason why renunciates and monasteries prevailed at that time. We were also shown why such positive changes would continue, and how for thousands of years to come, enlightenment would become increasingly easier to attain. Now, in this age, we are lucky to have such a swift, predictable technique.

Do you see, it's not that we *must* meditate? Rather, we *get* to meditate to improve and expand our lives.

COMMITMENT

Our initial commitment to meditation is generally fifteen to twenty minutes, twice a day. (Before breakfast and before dinner.) Like a twice-a-day antibiotic prescription, one daily pill might not produce the cure.[8] Following the prescribed course is essential. Disagree? Discuss your disagreement with your teacher. (I told my flight instructor how I liked a certain faster plane. His unforgettable response: "If you just learned to fly *this* plane straight and level it would be as fast as the other plane.") Same goes for our spiritual life.

Skilled meditation, like excelling at tennis, baseball, or golf, requires regularity, practice, and follow-through

---

[8] A word of caution: any attempt to substitute pills, chemicals, hypnosis, or the like, for a meditation program will result in a temporarily distorted impression of the truth, making it all the more challenging to achieve the high consciousness we long for.

for progress. I use the word "progress" because more than a few of the many Masters I visited corrected me when I mentioned "success," and "enlightenment." They advised that while *loving* God speeds the process, *striving* for the destination of "success" or "enlightenment" negatively affects our progress. "Place the goal in your heart, and then surrender without striving to achieve it. Just patiently and methodically immerse yourself in the silent beauty of the journey," was their advice.

SIX-MONTH CHECKUPS

Our regular, twice-daily meditation practice becomes not only a joy but also increasingly fulfilling as we are continually rewarded and amazed. Checking our progress every six months, we recognize and realize our growth. The enhancement of our spiritual nature shines as clearly in us as the reduction of falsity—falsity we never realized was painfully present, falsity that obscured the beauty and wonder of our own pure, Divine presence.

We return to our program excited and curious about what delusions will fall away next. We grow in vibrancy and depth like a cloth becoming more and more colorful as it is repetitively dipped in a very subtle dye. All the

Masters advised that enlightenment (*moksha*) is where we gently aim our intention, and then we follow the path of our teacher. "Do nothing to leave the path."

TRANSFORMATION

Accordingly, the divine Grace of enlightenment becomes a certainty as you cultivate inner stillness, and allow all your negativity, all that's not really you, to fall away. As Michelangelo so eloquently stated: "I saw the angel in the marble and carved until I set him free." Another way of saying he carved away everything that wasn't the angel.

The result we seek is to metaphorically amplify the brightness of our hibernating fifty-watt soul to one thousand watts or more. And to dim the flashy thousand-watt mind-ego to two hundred watts.

Imagine two projectors, each projecting a different image upon the same screen. One projector, representing the dominant mind-ego, has a one thousand-watt lamp projecting a human on a screen twenty feet away, while the second projector, representing the less dominant soul, has a fifty-watt lamp projecting a flower on the same screen.

Everything else being equal, which picture are we

going to see on the screen—the human or the flower? Sure, the human. The less dominant fifty-watt flower (soul) is totally overwhelmed by the thousand-watt, dominant picture of the human (mind-ego).

Dimming the mind-ego projector to two hundred watts and brightening the fifty-watt flower projector to a dominant one thousand watts reverses the result—the flower now overwhelms the human image.

With the dominant soul-flower outshining the body's dim light, the effect on the soul would be minimal if its body (container) died. If the body, mind-ego were dominant at the time of its death, we would expect the soul to experience more contrast by the death than if the soul had been dominant. Either way, the soul is always shining and untouched. Follow?

Now, which picture would we see if we turned the mind-ego projector off? Hmmm, pretty consistent with "life after death," don't you think?

AWAKENING

The physical body becomes sacred and devotional during the quieting process, allowing our soul to awaken from its hibernation. Once its divine presence becomes obvious, it grows to dominate what's left of the ego. Yet, the ego never completely disappears—more accurately, it thins.

Imagine we're inside a balloon that's being inflated. At the beginning we can't see beyond the thick rubber of the balloon. Yet as it inflates and thins we begin to see through and beyond the balloon. Eventually the balloon will become so thin that as we adjust our vision we are no longer aware of its presence.

My dear readers, all these metaphors demonstrate how this is only the beginning! As we practice our *sadhana* (overall spiritual practice), countless mystical experiences arrive to expand our consciousness, maturing it to higher and higher levels.

As the soul awakens, it's real…there is no "mood making." Our evolving glory of *Being*—the profound unconditional love, the magic of the real *here and now,* and its gift of natural knowing—is irresistibly charming. The contagious benefits course through our Being, illuminating our life and the lives of everyone around us.

I'm not saying this for the first time—I've spent a lifetime confirming we can trust the process. It replicates, and it's Divine. As humans become human *Beings,* we usher in the changes that will not only satisfy, but set us free. As we personally become thoroughly established and comfortable within this silent, transcendent state, we do not lose our immersion in bliss when returning to our everyday life in the everyday world.

And, remember that regularly slipping into Cosmic Consciousness unleashes certain powers that are progressively just right for your situation and your continued growth.

The World Needs You

So, you see now, the world is only half alive. It's not running late. It's right on time and eager to receive normalized, enlightened human Beings. We are becoming the change we want to see in the world. *It* has made our enlightenment contagious, benefiting everyone and everything. It has not always been this way.

Enlightenment—expanding exponetially—illminates the darkness as everything false falls away, nonviolently.

Awakening is spectacularly creative. It brings new and better ideas to obsolete the old, just as automobiles obsoleted the horse and buggy. Without coercion or threats, "obsoleting" offers nonviolent, gracefully evolving change—it transforms!

CHAPTER EIGHT

MEDITATING WITH YOUR MANTRA

A mantra is a sacred sound, usually a Sanskrit word or phrase that conveys one or more of the many names of God. A mantra is sacred because Divine Consciousness is inherent within the sound, providing it with a powerful and exquisitely uplifting quality that alters the climate of our mind and brightens our heart. The repetitive expression of such ancient sounds during meditation triggers soul memory as it quiets the mind and its comparing, judging, foolish inner dialog.

THE ORIGIN OF MANTRAS

Sacred mantras are over ten thousand years old and were initially perceived by ancient Rishis as Sanskrit invocations of the One. Just as Newton discovered the law of gravity but didn't invent it, the Rishis intuited these primordial sounds from that infinite ocean of Divine Energy we've named *It*. They then conveyed these sounds to their students for use as mantras, paving a direct path into the Divine, Itself. As mantras are precise and have always existed in a latent state as powerful energies, they cannot be tailor-made for us.

ACTIVATING YOUR MANTRA

The secret to mantras is they are "coded." They come alive when they are activated in one of two ways. The first method of activation occurs naturally, through repetition and devotion, and through deeper and deeper feeling and experience. The second way has to do with *diksha*.

The tantric tradition teaches that a mantra will be most powerful from the very beginning if it is given to you with diksha, the divine energy of a teacher and lineage of teachers through whom it is kept enlivened and empowered. In this way the mantra's Divine Consciousness and its codes and secrets are unlocked and ready to work for you. By receiving and accepting your mantra in this way, you instantaneously take it into your heart as part of you. You can acquire such a sacred mantra from me, or from another teacher qualified to instill the sacred sound into your heart with sacred energy.

If your mantra is not given to you with diksha (in a short ritual or ceremony of divine grace, at the least), it will probably take six months or longer to travel to your heart. You will probably experience it first on the lips and tongue, then the back of the mouth around the soft palate, and then in the throat. Finally, the feeling of pronouncing the mantra disappears as it enters the magnificent silence of your heart.

Use the mantra you are given by your teacher (guru). Don't change that mantra until your teacher tells you how, and under what circumstances, to use another mantra. Follow precisely the meditation instructions you are given.

Once you attain and regularly experience Cosmic Consciousness, you can afford to experiment and decide what works best for the new you. Until you are well established in Cosmic Consciousness, you will speed your progress if you follow the traditional path you are given.

THE MEANING OF THOUGHTS

The sacred consciousness of the mantra is the primary tool we use to quiet the mind and ego. Thoughts are attention grabbers. If we start our meditation with the intention "not to think," we create even more thoughts than usual, attracting what we don't want, in this case, just more thoughts. (Translated mantras will also attract what we don't want—a translation simply isn't coded with divine vibration. Using the original Sanskrit, in accordance with the science of sound, is essential. By using a powerful ancient mantra having to do with the presence or name of the Divine, Itself, we align with, and get, exactly that presence.)

Newcomers to meditation inevitably feel disappointed when thoughts prevent them from thinking their mantra. There are times when thoughts are so numerous and pressurized they dominate our precious twenty minutes. Just know that thoughts are a sign of unstressing. Yes, it would be nice not to have thoughts. But during meditation our stress takes the *form* of thoughts bubbling up to be released. With patience and perseverance, sooner or later not one bubble, not one thought, will remain.

You might think of stress like bubbles in a soda bottle. Take the bottle off the shelf and open it—no foam. Shake it and open it—it foams with pressurized bubbles. Same with your mantra. If you meditate following hours of balanced activity, your mantra will be more available during meditation than if you have been in an intense competitive environment.

The mantra does the work, not you, so just sit comfortably, repeat the mantra until you notice you've lost it, then innocently restore it.

A note to the ambitious: enlightenment is not attained by repeating your mantra a certain number of times. So there is no reason to be disappointed by the fact that you "forget" your mantra over and over during your meditation, and sometimes hardly get to it at all. You actually don't "forget." Once you start your mantra, it subtly keeps running even when obscured by pop-up thoughts, as clouds temporarily block the sun.

BREATHING TECHNIQUES

Pranayama (pronounced prahna yahm), the science of breath, is used for regulating and restraining the function of breathing.

Control of the breath is a very powerful technique that helps the inner workings of the body bring its mind under control—meaning, control the breath and what follows is basically automatic.

There are plenty of books and articles on breathing techniques, all of which agree it's helpful to consider a rule or two on the subject of breath management. I'm not discussing those rules here. You need to discuss them with a qualified teacher who has been taught by a Master with a lineage. You can read about breathing techniques, but you assume a risk that might be greater than the reward if you self-prescribe them. They won't always be harmful—sometimes they will protect you by shutting down your progress. I don't believe everyone who speaks or writes on pranayama. I'm exceedingly cautious. You might choose to be as well.

Pranayama Deemed Safe by Tradition

During your meditation you might breathe in rhythm with each mantra you repeat internally. Mantra—breathe-in, mantra—breathe out, mantra—breathe in, mantra—breathe out....Continue until your forget about it.

Another technique is to move your awareness of the breath around until you find a location with which you're most comfortable. Feel the breath as it enters and passes around the opening of each nostril. Or, feel it curve around the back of the nose and down the throat by the soft palate. Or, feel the breath as it goes through the bronchial tubes at the top of the lungs. Focusing your attention on your breath is a good way to reduce or postpone thoughts from distracting you from your mantra.

Noticing your attention is following a thought can be your clue to gently replace the thought with your mantra. Restart the mantra as gently as you lost it.

Note: All your mental focus, and your concern over breathing rhythms, naturally falls away each time you transcend into the silence beyond thought.

The sky now sees
in me all the stars I
see in it.

Daniel Ladinsky

CHAPTER NINE

ENTRAINING THE SACRED INTO OUR LIVES

The mantra you will be using in meditation entrains the mind as it amplifies your soul into the One Divine Consciousness.

MAGNETS

"Entrain" is a key word—it is the very "coding" we seek. Entrainment is the process used to create a magnet from a piece of ordinary steel. The steel bar becomes a magnet as it's repeatedly stroked in one direction by a magnet! The bar is entrained by the influence and character of the magnet's tried and true energy. In only a few minutes, the steel bar exhibits the properties of the entraining magnet itself.

Just the influence of a stroking magnet over the bar creates a new magnet. Surrendering to our own sacred practices creates a sacred practitioner. Magnet makes magnet. Sacred makes sacred!

Can you appreciate how a sacred mantra works to entrain us, just as the magnet's specific energy works to magnetize? Our presence needs only to be exposed repeatedly over time to "sacred sound" in order to entrain and align our mind to become one with our strengthening soul.

METHODS OF OFFERING MANTRAS

Entraining ourselves sacred is accomplished by a variety of practices. At the center of many of them is the repetition of sacred mantras—aloud, or silently in the heart.

In Chapter Ten you will be given a sacred mantra. If you accept that mantra to guide you into the Divine, it becomes your sacred meditation mantra.

Your meditation depends on your personal, powerful sacred mantra as your primary tool. During meditation that mantra is repeated internally. Walking mantras, *japa*, chanting, and call-and-response chanting (*kirtan*), are four other methods for offering mantras. They are usually practiced with mantras other than your meditation mantra. When we're with others who are chanting our meditation mantra aloud, there is no objection to joining in. Occasionally we might want to do a *mala* (a string of 108 beads) or so to Shiva (Sanskrit for Pure Consciousness within everything). In that case vocal repetition of your meditation mantra is also appropriate.

WALKING MANTRAS are usually repeated while doing anything physical—for example, walking, doing dishes, raking leaves, driving in light traffic, or just passing time when we are not doing anything with our mind that might interfere. Such sacred mantra repetition is a great tool to improve our outlook on life while it enlivens the sacred physical we are entraining.

I would prefer you not use your meditation mantra as a walking mantra. My favorite walking mantra is *Ham Sa* (I am One with the Divine). The in-breath whispers "Ham" (*hahm*) and the out-breath whispers "Sa" (*sah*). And yes, another version (same meaning) of this mantra is *So Ham*—breathe in "So" and breathe out "Ham," in a most natural in and out whisper or inaudibly. I have inquired of many Masters and have been repeatedly assured that either version works equally well. Just choose the one that feels most natural and stick with it. Ham Sa or So Ham.

Use this mantra anytime you want, so long as it

does not conflict with any other traditional practice. Innocently—without expectations—let the mantra do the work.

JAPA is the repetition of mantras aloud or internally with a 108-bead mala. Japa is not ordinarily practiced while meditating since meditation is a separate technique of its own. Japa is a form of prayer, often offered to a specific god or goddess, each a unique aspect of the Divine. Japa colors the heart to match the vibes of the chosen deity—in other words it allows us to "grok" the deity.

Grok means to understand so thoroughly that the observed becomes a part of the observer. It's not difficult. Just choose a *murti*,[9] picture, flower, or candle, and gaze at it. Gazing is accomplished by watching the object, and while maintaining your attention, adjusting your focus in front of or beyond the object. The object becomes a little blurry, but it's your attention that now is watching it.

Just sit quietly, gazing for a minute or two and the

------

[9] Any figure, image, statue, or embodiment of the Divine in a place of worship.

object will morph (vary in form). Sometimes you'll notice you are watching the object through a smoky haze.

Once it morphs, notice what's happening in your heart. Notice how you feel. Your heart is connecting with the object, and the more sensitive you are, the more you can know it intimately—from the inside out.

Now that you know how to grok, you know how to connect with and deeply worship a murti. The murti is the embodiment of the aspect's Divine energy. Whatever aspect of the Divine you worship, grok it, and ... when you open to the truth (the murti's energy), you become the truth (the murti's energy entrains you). Worshiping is more than loving and respecting the object. It's devoting your heart to it, groking it, *sharing* love between you. Thou art That—"That," is that aspect's consciousness. Such sharing acts to entrain.

I also use my mala for timely mantras that carry divine blessings for nature, serious illness, death, or inviting healing.

CHANTING (non-musical repetition) is done aloud. The chanted mantra reverberates through the body and is particularly effective at opening and enlivening the heart chakra. It is a profound technique to settle us into the *Bhava* (or *bhav*, Sanskrit for feelings of absorption into the Divine) by accessing the Divine Feminine with all its feelings of divine tenderness.

KIRTAN is call-and-response chanting to music. Chanting to music for thirty to forty minutes a week is a loving practice, a very powerful tool, and it's extremely entraining. Buy a CD of your favorite chant or kirtan artist and turn up the volume. Sing the chant with all your heart while you move and clap to the music. Notice the ecstatic effect it has on your mind, heart, and soul.

Not to be missed is the adventure of kirtan chanting at various yoga and spiritual centers. You will likely have a deep, powerful experience with a whole room full of people joyously moving and singing, and obviously enjoying the bhav. Some of today's kirtan performances have made it into the top ten in popular music. (If Krishna Das comes to town, you may just find us in the audience!)

Kirtan sessions satisfy satsang, japa, mantra, and chanting, all at the same time.

Look what's happening. Once mysterious, hidden,

and misunderstood, the spiritual path has become the new adventure. Expanding consciousness is indeed contagious, sparking many new and shared spiritual practices.

MORE ENTRAINMENT

Other practices that entrain minds and hearts with the sacred:

- *Satsang* (meeting with a spiritual group) is the Sanskrit word for "gathering together with the Divine." Spend time in the company of God-minded persons, persons of similar sacred interest and intent.

- *Bestowing grace.* Bless your food before you partake. Some blessings serve to cleanse food of its accumulated stress while other blessings *sanctify* food, creating alchemy as they turn your food into a grateful gift or offering back to God. This gift returns to you as you consume the food.

- *Sacred food preparation.* Another method of entraining and sanctifying food is to sing or chant sacred mantras as you mentally infuse them into the food while stirring or blending your ingredients. Blessings in every bite!

- *Yoga breathing.* Regulating and restraining the function of breath (*pranayama*, or "science of breath") helps to quiet the mind. This is an advanced technique that deserves discussion with your trusted teacher before adding it to your program. I recommend appropriate techniques at the appropriate time.

- *Working with a Master.* A Master has Divine authority to bestow grace and thereby accelerate the enlightenment process. A soul can be further nourished and entrained by the Pure Energy of an already awakened soul wisely guiding a worthy aspirant further and further past impediments and obstacles all the way into the enlightened state—home. He or she serves as a very powerful magnet, and entraining with a proper Master will require fewer "passes over the steel" than working on one's own. Enlightenment is contagious. As an "enlightener" or remover of darkness, a Master (guru) arrives when you are ready.

- *Personalized ritual.* Over time you, and your inner guru, will cultivate an order and rhythm of mantras, meditation, chanting, and study that is distinctly your own. You will naturally be drawn to the steppingstones it places one at a time for you to follow to your own union with the Divine. Trust, and follow your heart while you remain within the rules of purity of your tradition.

- *Laughter.* I notice when we experience something together that's spontaneously funny—simultaneous laughter imparts a flash of Unity. Diana and I frequently notice the occurrence. Shared enthusiasm also creates a remarkable, although different, experience.

A Sacred Day

As we pass from one phase of our lives into the next, our commitments and opportunities shift. By age fifty-five, plus or minus five years, our children are most likely grown, and the business of living has settled so we can take more time for ourselves. For me it felt like the wind was at my back. I had grown to love my spiritual practice—the more I did my practice the more I loved it. I wanted to devote more time to experience the depths of spiritual silence. I worked out my own program, a program that, as time allows, I adjust.

Now, most days begin for me when I naturally awaken around 3 a.m. (Most people might not recognize this as a divine impulse to begin one's day. Most would label it insomnia, feel frustrated, and stare at the ceiling for an hour or so before falling asleep, and then wake up tired.) But I find the morning hours energizing for meditating and devotion. According to yogic tradition, one and a half hours before sunrise is a time called *brahma-muhurta*, a period considered especially powerful for spiritual activity.

Shortly before dawn, I accept the invitation, weather allowing, to step outdoors and appreciate the moonlight while I choose a flower from our garden to place on our altar in gratitude for the grace I continue to receive. I then light a candle flame before one of the aspects of the Divine I choose to align with, and often include a one, two, or three mala japa to internalize that deity and sweeten my heart. Using the candle flame, I ignite the end of a stick of incense and reverently wave it around the room as a gesture of purification and then extinguish it. (Our "meditory" is so small that we'd have to call 911 if we burned a whole stick of incense with the door closed.)

When I have finished offering gratitude, I wrap myself in three yards of silk to hold the energy in, and for warmth. If it's chilly, I add more wraps to my silk cocoon. I then meditate by closing my eyes, withdrawing the senses, and starting my mantra.

Just as we all wait for a few minutes before sleep comes, when we're meditating we wait for the body to let go and then transcend. When I return to bed, usually within an hour and a half, I fall into a profoundly deep slumber. Since transcending is regarded as deeper rest than sleep, it's not surprising to wake up at 7 a.m. fully rested.

I often set aside certain three or four hour-long periods to chant, meditate, and worship with gratitude.

As the years click by, my devotion and joy in the process has only increased. Love...I've never experienced such profound deep love for everything! I find I focus my ever-expanding love on my fabulous wife and divine partner, Diana. The more complete my love for Diana, the more I can love the universe. Love and loving intimately as husband and wife, compares well to sunshine and sunshine through a magnifying glass. Adjust that glass and the sunshine makes things smoke. Adjust your love for one another and the energy becomes sweet and velvety. My family, close friends, and beloved students all benefit.

Joy and bliss constantly underlie all my activity. Sometimes I feel so full of the Divine I inwardly repeat mantras of gratitude and thanks.

Sacred practices are continuous throughout the day. Blessing food, chanting in the car, meditation after work, bedtime prayers of thanks.

Gratitude and consciousness expand—hand in hand.

CHAPTER TEN

YOUR MANTRA

The experience of transcendence can transport us into the highest meditative states one can experience. What follows is some of the best, time-tested spiritual information on attaining God realization.

INITIATION

I'm often asked about initiation in spiritual pursuits.

Truly, there is usually no need for a formal initiation in spiritual matters. In divine reality, our initiation takes place the moment we make a personal decision to accept or experience a Master or a mantra or anything of a spiritual nature. Our personal acceptance triggers our heart and soul to respond, and like a seed, to absorb nourishment.

If It's Not Easy, We're Not Doing It Right

Learning the art of meditation is far easier than learning to ride a bike. Like riding a bike, we can't learn how to do it from a book, we can only grab the bike and hop on—over and over again—until we're riding it—it eventually becomes second nature. And, like riding a bike, meditation requires persistence, for it's persistence that opens the door to our soul. As we look back every six months to see the changes, persistence pays off. Yet unlike riding a bike, meditation is effortless.

Example of Meditating on a Good Day

Meditation can be thought of as a mechanical process. Sitting comfortably, we (as experienced meditators) settle in for thirty seconds to a minute and then gently introduce (become aware of) our mantra. At first, thoughts drown out the mantra and our substitution of mantra for thoughts plays out back and forth for a bit. After a few minutes we notice the reduction of thoughts and increasing silence as the mantra gradually withdraws our attention from the senses and the ideas on which they focus.

A few more minutes into it, our mantra settles us into transcendence, a super-conscious state where the mind, body, and intellect have been silenced, revealing the borders of Being.

Once deeply transcended and absorbed into Being, the sweet, pure silence of the Divine, we are clear of our senses, and solely within the heart—a transcendent experience I described earlier as the fourth state, or turiya.

If we were to have the capability to maintain turiya as we gently awaken from our meditation, we would find ourselves on the threshold of Cosmic Consciousness, the fifth state and the first level of enlightenment. Instead, coming out brings with it a sudden return of our senses that overwhelms our transcendent experience. While we are very relaxed, creative, alert, and often blissed-out, we have returned to the normal awareness of the waking state. In time, the return of the senses becomes increasingly gentle, so we can remain in the transcendental state for increasing lengths of time following meditation.

WELCOME TO YOUR MANTRA

You now have a broad base of information, which makes this a good time to introduce you to your meditation mantra.

Mantras used to be kept secret, so secret it wouldn't have been appropriate to publish them. Those days disappeared with the birth of the Internet. You can now easily find a myriad of mantras in books and online.

The mantra I'm about to disclose is available to you elsewhere. But matching a mantra, receiving instructions for use within its tradition, and having the mantra delivered with diksha—such can be regarded as an important find.

I have deeply researched mantras. There are literally thousands, but only a few make sense for meditation. Rule of thumb: we will come to be whatever we meditate upon. Meditating on the names of God amplifies our Divine Nature. One of the most powerful and popular mantras focuses on Shiva, the Sanskrit name for Divine Consciousness.

Let me explain. In Chapter One, I described how the Divine was divided into male and female, and how the male aspect, Shiva, is Pure Consciousness, and the female aspect, Shakti, is all action and form.

All of us spend our waking hours engaging in action and form with Shakti, the Divine Feminine. We want to spend quality time with Pure Consciousness as well

(the very basis of who we are, but so different from our everyday awareness.)

GREAT MANTRA

Om Namah Shivaya is the mantra. It is a mantra used by *all* of the Masters we interviewed in India. I've been using Om Namah Shivaya as a meditation mantra for twenty years. Ten years ago I asked my Great Master, Shree Maa, if I should be using a more advanced mantra than Om Namah Shivaya. Shree Maa is always polite, and she simply told me that the nature of Om Namah Shivaya is so pure and relevant that she still uses it (among others) daily. So do I.

Let's take it apart and see why this mystical mantra is so perfect. "Om" is the infinte beyond conception. "Namah" is translated as "I bow down." And "Shivaya," I'll discuss in a minute, but first we have to finish with "Namah." Although "Namah" is literally translated as "I bow down," this is not the best translation for Western usage. In the West, when we hear "I bow down," we hear "I submit to." A better translation for usage in the United States, is "I honor you, or I *align* with you," similar to what our shaking hands is supposed to achieve.

Hearing Namah, its meaning goes to our hearts, inviting and accepting a connection to become one with the Divine.

Now, let's discuss "Shivaya." This name of God offers a friendly, intimate invitation to salute, align with, and merge into Shiva's Energy of Infinite Goodness—Pure Consciousness—contained in everyone and everything. The light (Divine Energy) of this Shivaya mantra, amplifies and strengthens the soul as it destroys all darkness and removes all sins and impurities of the heart. Repetition of this great name intimately invites us to grok, and become one with Divine Consciousness—the Consciousness we experience as ageless and infinite within our heart. How better to awaken our true nature?

Om, the primordial sound of the universe + Namah, I align with + Shivaya, Pure Consciousness, becomes: "With the sound of the universe, I intimately align my heart to merge with Divine Consciousness."

All worded in Sanskrit, this simple mantra is more powerful and esoterically complex than we can imagine. There are scientific and mathematical reasons that make this mantra *perfect*. If you are interested in learning more about it, there are many books documenting the perfection of Om Namah Shivaya. Surely, hundreds of thousands of words have been written in its favor.

MEDITATION INSTRUCTIONS

So now, sit in a quiet place and take in the mantra. (If you like, you can go to our website to hear the mantra's correct pronunciation and timing.) You can sit to meditate using the mantra for fifteen to twenty minutes, two sessions a day, for a few weeks. Once you're comfortable, you can meditate for twenty minutes—no more than thirty minutes—twice a day. After the first year you can do whatever amount of time feels comfortable, but *no more* than one hour, twice a day without special instructions from your teacher. After six months you qualify to receive carefully selected pranayama techniques that will add to your program.

YOUR MEDITATION PLACE AND SEAT

Begin by choosing a quiet, comfortable, indoor place where you will not be disturbed or distracted by sounds and activity for thirty minutes or so. Perhaps you will choose to sit on a chair or a floor cushion in your bedroom, a den, or even a spare closet. Meditating in your regular place and posture is a method of enhancing and absorbing the accumulating Shakti generated during your devotion.

Before starting your mantra, sit comfortably and, if possible, in your place, your usual seat, and in the following posture. If sitting on a chair, place your feet flat on the floor with legs parallel and hip-width apart. Settle your sitting bones into the seat and gently elongate your spine. If you are sitting on a cushion on the floor, assume a comfortable cross-legged posture, or the posture you usually enjoy for meditation. During meditation it's best to keep your spine long, your shoulders soft, and your head lightly floating with chin very slightly lowered. Notice how extending your chest further lengthens your spine.

Cover or wrap yourself in a length of silk or a meditation shawl, creating a cozy cocoon that will contain your Shakti, keep you warm, and protect you from drafts. Relax deeply as you set your intention to be fully open and present.

You might place your hands on your thighs, palms down, in *chin mudra* (with the *tips* of each thumb and index finger touching). Palms may be up when you wish to open to the energy of your teacher.

Place Your Awareness on Your Breath

Gently closing your eyes—become aware of your breath.

Extend exhalations a little longer as you relax all muscles in your face and jaw. Notice that your body becomes more and more relaxed, and your mind enters a state of alertness and attunement.

Your entire Being is ready to relax into Divine transcendence as you begin repetition of your mantra, "Om Namah Shivaya."

On the in-breath, "Om Namah Shivaya."

On the out-breath "Om Namah Shivaya."

On the in-breath "Om Namah Shivaya…"

As we transcend into the safety of our heart we naturally forget our breathing pattern, and ride on the natural breath, deep or shallow, as we merge into Divine silence.

Continue for fifteen or twenty minutes.

Returning

When you are complete, sing softly from your heart, Om *Shanti, Shanti, Shanti* (peace, peace, peace). Wait for a minute or two while you take a moment to open your eyes, wiggling your fingers and toes to bring your attention back into your body and the world. It's best to emerge gently before returning to activity.

Note: Should your meditation be interrupted by a phone call or someone at the door, once you have handled the interruption, even if it wasn't too lengthy, it might be best if you returned for five minutes of settling, and then come out of meditation in normal fashion.

Because the object of meditation is to withdraw from the senses, it's not helpful to meditate before a colorful sunset or a beautiful scene in nature; our intention is to withdraw from the field of action and the senses. Choose a secluded location where you can practice regularly.

SITTING UPRIGHT

If we're intending to go to sleep, we would lie down with the intention of sleeping and just innocently wait for sleep. If we are intending to meditate, we sit comfortably with the back straight and with the intention of dropping into transcendental Consciousness. With a goal in our heart and trust in the body to let go, our attention innocently follows the mantra as it does it's thing to clear the way to a field of absolute stillness and Being—the kingdom of God within.